EXTREME RAINFOREST

KINGFISHER
LONDON & NEW YORK

Published in the United States by Kingfisher,
175 Fifth Ave., New York, NY 10010
Kingfisher is an imprint of Macmillan Children's Books, London.
All rights reserved.

Distributed in the U.S. by Macmillan,
175 Fifth Ave., New York, NY 10010
Distributed in Canada by H.B. Fenn and Company Ltd.,
34 Nixon Road, Bolton, Ontario L7E 1W2

WELDON OWEN INC.
CEO, President Terry Newell
VP, Sales and New Business Development Amy Kaneko

VP, Publisher Roger Shaw
Executive Editor Mariah Bear
Editor Lucie Parker
Project Editors Nam Nguyen, Sarah Hines Stephens
Editorial Assistant Emelie Griffin

Associate Creative Director Kelly Booth
Senior Designer William Mack
Assistant Designer Michel Gadwa

Production Director Chris Hemesath
Production Manager Michelle Duggan
Color Manager Teri Bell

Library of Congress Cataloging-in-Publication data has been applied for.

ISBN: 978-0-7534-6665-0

Kingfisher books are available for special promotions and premiums.
For details contact: Special Markets Department, Macmillan, 175 Fifth Ave., New York, NY 10010.

For more information, please visit www.kingfisherbooks.com

A Weldon Owen Production
415 Jackson Street
San Francisco, California 94111

Printed in Shenzhen, China, by Asia Pacific Offset.
5 4 3 2 1
2011 2012 2013 2014 2015

EXTREME
RAINFOREST

KINGFISHER
NEW YORK

CONTENTS

MEET THE BEASTS

Rainforests cover only 6 percent of Earth's surface, yet they support more than half of the world's plant and animal species. In this wet and often unstable environment, how do the sneaky creatures creeping on the forest floor, the amazing animals lurking in plant pools, and the large beasts navigating the treacherous treetops adapt for survival? Toxic skin, poison-injecting fangs, sonic muscles, and hidden wings are just a few of the astounding tools that rainforest animals have at their disposal. Even so, thriving on the leafy forest floor or in the branches of this high-rise habitat is no picnic. Step into the rainforest and see for yourself.

MIRACLE WALKER

Brilliant green and equipped with flashing tails, sharp claws, and plumelike crests of skin crowning their heads, basilisk lizards stand out in the rainforest crowd. These dazzling reptiles also have a skill that no other animals of their size possess: when pursued, they can run on water, leaving enemies to eat their dust—or rather, their spray.

GEOGRAPHY
Southern Mexico through Central America to Ecuador

HABITAT
Streaks past dense vegetation, shrubs, and trees near water

GREEN BASILISK LIZARD
Basiliscus plumifrons

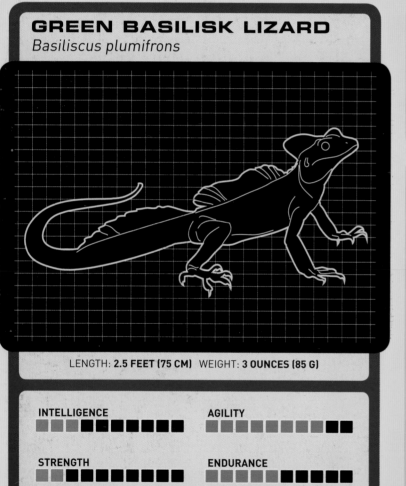

LENGTH: **2.5 FEET (75 CM)**   WEIGHT: **3 OUNCES (85 G)**

INTELLIGENCE

AGILITY

STRENGTH

ENDURANCE

SPEED

EVASION

PREY

GRASSHOPPERS
Basilisk lizards hunt near the base of trees and on the ground, looking to snare juicy grasshoppers.

ENEMY

HEADING FOR DANGER
When hanging out on the forest floor, away from watery escape routes, basilisk lizards risk being hunted by snakes. These slithery predators often swallow lizards headfirst to avoid getting scratched.

FLYING FLAGS
The males' bright, fanning head crests attract females on the lookout for a mate.

BALANCE BEAM
Lizards' tails make up 18 percent of their weight. The tails provide counterbalance and keep lizards upright while running.

SUPERPOWER
Water walking
EQUIPMENT
Long, thin tail; sharp, climbing claws; wide, slapping feet
WEAKNESS
Large size (big basilisks are too slow to run far over water)
FACT
Basilisks can swim well in water when they tire of running on it.

HANGING HOOKS
Sharp claws on each foot grip

COOL TREADS
Long, spread-out toes create enough force to propel lizards across water at speeds of up to 7 miles (11 km) per hour.

SUPERPOWERS
Crushing jaws; extreme agility

EQUIPMENT
Powerful legs; large paws

WEAKNESS
Extreme self-confidence (jaguars often walk out in the open, making themselves easy targets)

FACT
Most jaguars are yellow with black spots, but the black jaguar's skin contains more melanin, which makes it darker.

HEADLIGHTS
A reflective layer in the back of the eye doubles the available light, boosting the jaguar's vision in dim conditions.

MIGHTY COMPACTOR
Large, dense jaws kill by crushing the skulls or shattering the necks of prey with a single bite.

CRUISING ZONE
Jaguars patrol a territory of up to 60 square miles (155 sq km). Male cats refuse to share turf with other males.

CAN OPENERS
Thirty sharp teeth are the perfect tools for breaking turtle shells, gnawing holes in scaled caimans, and prying apart prey.

GEOGRAPHY

Mexico through Central America to northern Argentina

HABITAT

Patrols tropical forests, deciduous forests, savannas, and scrublands

DARK STALKER

Black jaguars eat anything that moves, from snails to deer. These densely built predators have thick legs, large feet, and strong jaws, perfectly suited to their powerful attacks. At home in the trees or swimming the flooded rainforest, jaguars are extremely intelligent: they're the only big cats clever enough to tackle prey as well-armored as turtles and caimans.

ENEMY

POACHERS

Poachers kill jaguars as well as many of their food sources. There may be as few as 15,000 or so of these beautiful cats left in the wild.

PREY

CAPYBARAS

Jaguars are big cats, so it makes sense that they like to eat large rodents. Capybaras weigh as much as 140 pounds (65 kg).

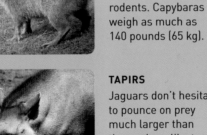

TAPIRS

Jaguars don't hesitate to pounce on prey much larger than themselves, like tapirs, which measure up to 8 feet (2.5 m) long.

CAIMANS

Jaguars hunt caimans and crack their tough armor by chewing through the caimans' sides, where there are no protective scales.

BLACK JAGUAR
Panthera onca

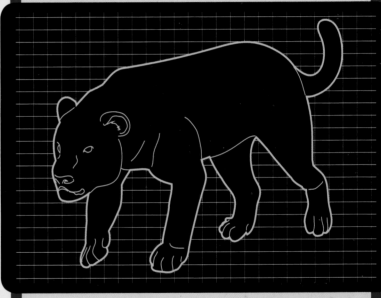

LENGTH: **5 FEET (1.5 M)** WEIGHT: **150 POUNDS (70 KG)**

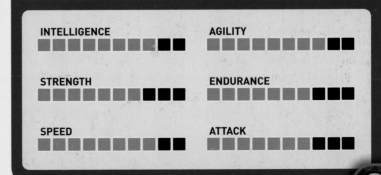

INTELLIGENCE

AGILITY

STRENGTH

ENDURANCE

SPEED

ATTACK

SUPER GENIUS

The brainiacs of the bird world, African gray parrots are famous for their smarts and astounding speaking ability. Sadly, since they only live in a small area of central and west Africa, and their intelligence makes them such attractive pets, they have become endangered by the people who illegally trap and sell them. Left in the wild, African grays learn their own language from their parents and live together in highly social groups.

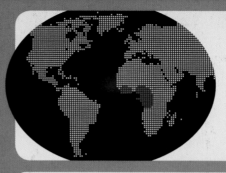

GEOGRAPHY
West and central Africa

HABITAT
Flocks in canopies of lowland rainforests

AFRICAN GRAY PARROT
Psittacus erithacus

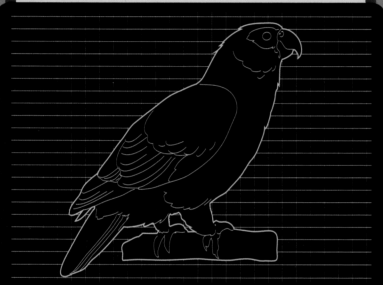

LENGTH: **13 INCHES (33 CM)**   WEIGHT: **1 POUND (0.45 KG)**

INTELLIGENCE
■■■■■■■■■■

AGILITY
■■■■■■■■■□

STRENGTH
■■■■□□□□□□

ENDURANCE
■■■□□□□□□□

SPEED
■■■□□□□□□□

EVASION
■■■■□□□□□□

ENEMY

PALM NUT VULTURES
These vultures have a favorite food in common with African grays—palm nut seeds. The bullies are often seen harassing parrot flocks in treetops.

TOOL TIME

BEAK BREAKER
African gray parrots use their sharp, ever-growing beaks and muscular, fingerlike tongues to position and crack nuts. Their beaks can grow strong enough to cut through wire fencing!

RAIN SLICKER
Preen glands secrete natural oils that parrots spread on their feathers to keep them supple and waterproof.

CAGE JAW
Parrots' upper jaws are reinforced with multiple strips of bone. These extra bone segments add strength and protect against impact.

HOOK MOUTH
A superelastic ligament attaches a parrot's upper beak and skull. The extra flexibility allows the bird to hook and slide along branches with its mouth.

SUPERPOWERS
Masterful mimicry; superior intelligence

EQUIPMENT
Powerful beak; flexible jaw

WEAKNESS
Takes 60 to 70 days for babies to leave the nest

FACT
Lacking vocal chords, African grays make sound by blowing across the tops of their airways.

SUPERPOWER
Extreme energy efficiency

EQUIPMENT
Three sharp claws; extra neck vertebrae; absorbent fur

WEAKNESS
Poor temperature control (dependent on warm environment)

FACT
Although awkward on land, sloths are excellent swimmers.

HANDY CLAWS
Three long claws on each leg are used for fighting off predators and hanging from tree limbs.

ABOUT-FACE
Sloths have extra neckbones, allowing them to turn their heads 270 degrees.

GREEN ENERGY
Sloth fur absorbs water and encourages the growth of algae, which provides both camouflage and nutrients.

COMB-OVER
Since sloths hang belly-up, their hair parts along their stomachs to direct rainwater off their bodies.

GEOGRAPHY
From south Central America to northern Argentina

HABITAT
Naps in mid- to upper-forest canopies

SLOW AND STEADY
Despite their reputation, sloths aren't lazy—they're just energy efficient. Their low metabolism and creeping pace make them well suited for life as large vegetarian mammals. By sleeping 20 out of 24 hours, and moving at an average speed of 1,000 feet (300 m) per hour, they expend fewer than 100 calories a day—less energy than is found in a slice of bread.

ENEMY

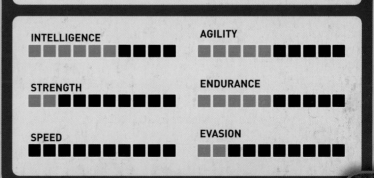

JAGUARS
Sloths are vulnerable to jaguar attacks on the ground, so they only descend from the trees to go to the bathroom every three to four days.

THREE-TOED SLOTH
Bradypus tridactylus

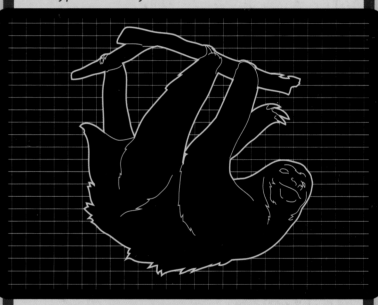

LENGTH: **2 FEET (60 CM)** WEIGHT: **11 POUNDS (5 KG)**

IN ACTION

COMMANDO CRAWL
Long, curved claws are great for hanging in trees but terrible for walking on land. To move on the ground, sloths crawl slowly and awkwardly—pulling themselves forward with their claws.

INTELLIGENCE	AGILITY
STRENGTH	ENDURANCE
SPEED	EVASION

NORTH AMERICA

The temperate, mossy rainforest of North America's Pacific Northwest boasts the coldest rainforest climate and the most ancient trees, along with landslides and avalanches.

WESTERN AFRICA

Once an unbroken expanse, Africa's rainforests are now solitary pockets on misty mountain islands. These islands receive less than two hours of sunlight during the rainy season.

SOUTH AMERICA

South America's rainforests cover nearly half the continent. They are the world's most diverse in spite of seasonal rains that flood forests up to 25 feet (7.5 m).

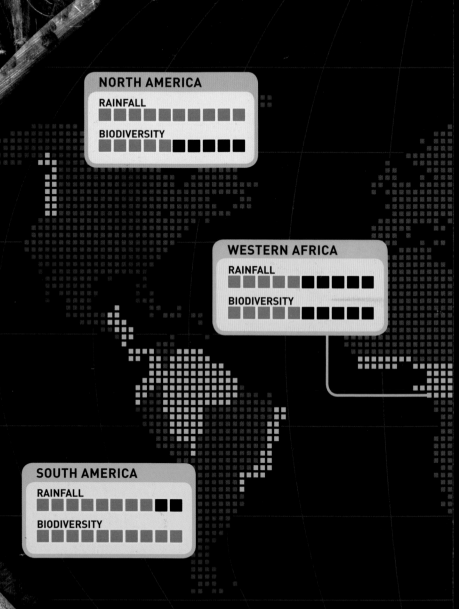

NORTH AMERICA
RAINFALL
BIODIVERSITY

WESTERN AFRICA
RAINFALL
BIODIVERSITY

SOUTH AMERICA
RAINFALL
BIODIVERSITY

RAINFORESTS OF THE WORLD

Whether it arrives during a wet season, comes in sporadic storms, or falls steadily year-round, an average annual rainfall between 8 and 15 feet (2.5–4.5 m) is what makes a rainforest a rainforest. Although they share other common traits, including dense tree canopies and amazing biodiversity (the variety of animals and plants they host), differences in climate and geography make each of the world's rainforests as unique as their plant and animal populations.

Asia is home to one-fourth of the world's rainforests. This dramatic region is subject to typhoons, monsoons, earthquakes, and, during periods of drought, even fires.

ASIA

RAINFALL

BIODIVERSITY

OCEANIA

Clusters of trees, rather than unbroken forest, characterize the dense rainforests that grow along Australia's western coast and across all of New Guinea.

OCEANIA

RAINFALL

BIODIVERSITY

MADAGASCAR

Madagascar's rainforests have developed in isolation from Africa for millions of years. Ninety percent of the island's plants and shrubs are found nowhere else on Earth.

MADAGASCAR

RAINFALL

BIODIVERSITY

KING OF THE HILL

Tamanduas, also known as lesser anteaters, may be smaller than their oversize cousins, but they are better adapted to living in rainforests. Unlike ground-dwelling giant anteaters, tamanduas can prowl both on the forest floor and in the trees, and they hunt after dark. They use their sharp sense of smell to track down meals at night, when termites are most active.

GEOGRAPHY
Venezuela to northern Argentina and Uruguay

HABITAT
Climbs among branches near water in rainforests and savannas

TAMANDUA
Tamandua tetradactyla

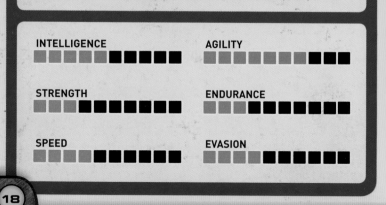

LENGTH: **3 FEET (1 M)**   WEIGHT: **11 POUNDS (5 KG)**

INTELLIGENCE

AGILITY

STRENGTH

ENDURANCE

SPEED

EVASION

PREY

TERMITES
Tamanduas are related to anteaters. They eat only ants and termites, preferring varieties that make their nests in the branches of trees.

TOOL TIME

FIGHTING STANCE
When threatened, tamanduas brandish their sharp claws like blades and use their tails as tripods to stand upright. In trees they hang by their tails—keeping their arms free for slashing.

CHEMICAL CLOUD
If threatened, tamanduas release a stench from glands below their tails that deters predators.

NOSE KNOWS
Supersensitive noses expertly sniff out ant and termite nests.

SUPERPOWER
Specialized night hunting

EQUIPMENT
Clawed feet; prehensile tail; long snout and tongue

WEAKNESS
Awkward walkers (must walk on heels due to long claws)

FACT
Tamanduas sweat only through their noses, lips, and toes.

SAFETY HARNESS
Tamanduas' grasping, prehensile tails are as long as their bodies and wrap around branches to hold them aloft while they hunt.

LINT ROLLER
The tamandua's tongue can grow up to 16 inches (40 cm) long. It is equipped with tiny spikes that snare termites.

INFRARED WEB
Heat-sensing pits are set at different angles to cast a wide sensory net—perfect for locating prey.

SUPERPOWERS
Camouflage; heat detection

EQUIPMENT
Infrared detectors; curved teeth; muscular body; prehensile tail

WEAKNESS
Weak eyesight (boas depend on scent and heat to track prey)

FACT
Emerald tree boas are born reddish-brown and turn green as they grow older.

MEAT HOOKS
Large front teeth are curved backward to embed deeper into struggling prey.

WHIP GRIP
Boas hang suspended from branches by their prehensile tails. They use their coils like ropes to descend on unwitting animals.

GEOGRAPHY
Venezuela to northern Bolivia and northern Brazil

HABITAT
Slithers in forest canopies, swamps, and rivers

THE BIG SQUEEZE
Emerald tree boas are beautiful by day, curled in the rainforest canopy. But by night, stealthily traveling through the treetops looking for dinner, they are decidedly deadly. Once boas locate their prey, they wrap it up in their long, muscular bodies and squeeze tighter and tighter, eventually killing the animal before eating it headfirst and whole.

PREY

TURNIP-TAILED GECKOS
Emerald boas kill lizards such as turnip-tailed geckos by constriction. Once the lizard stops breathing, the snake swallows it whole.

TOOL TIME

UP A TREE
Bright green boa scales are scattered with white markings. When boas lie coiled over branches in the rainforest canopy, their bodies look like leaves dappled with sunlight.

EMERALD TREE BOA
Corallus caninus

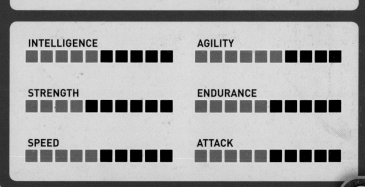

LENGTH: **6 FEET (2 M)**   DIAMETER: **2 INCHES (5 CM)**

INTELLIGENCE	AGILITY
STRENGTH	ENDURANCE
SPEED	ATTACK

MULTILEGGED MONSTER

Giant centipedes are the ultimate all-terrain terror. Their long, segmented bodies are lined with dozens of gripping legs, allowing them to stalk their next meal as easily from the ground as they can hanging from the ceiling of a cave. Once they sense their prey, centipedes attack with powerful fangs, injecting victims with lethal poison that stuns first, then kills.

GEOGRAPHY
Colombia, Venezuela, the Guianas, western Brazil

HABITAT
Creeps through soil, leaf litter, and rotten wood

GIANT CENTIPEDE
Scolopendra gigantea

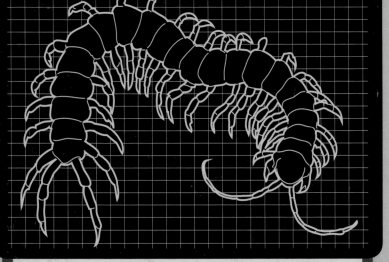

LENGTH: **10 INCHES (25 CM)** WEIGHT: **0.5 OUNCES (14 G)**

INTELLIGENCE
AGILITY
STRENGTH
ENDURANCE
SPEED
ATTACK

CENTIPEDE POISON
The centipede's two black-tipped fangs inject poison into its prey. This poison slows prey while the centipede wraps its many legs around it.

TOOL TIME

MICE
Mice and centipedes both live on the forest floor. If their paths cross, a mouse will likely get a lethal hug from its neighbor.

PREY

TOADS
Centipedes eat prey such as toads by biting the toads' necks to stun them, then eating their bodies down to their chests and bellies.

BATS
Using their rear legs to cling to cave roofs, centipedes dangle head-down in the dark to snare bats out of the air with their front feet.

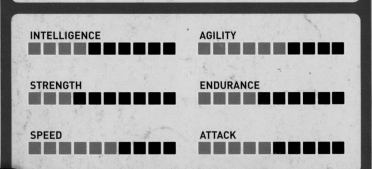

BIGHEARTED
Extremely long hearts run the length of giant centipedes' bodies.

SHARP TURNS
Segmented bodies bend to slip through crevices and coil around prey.

SUPERPOWERS
Flexibility; multilegged gripping action; deadly poison

EQUIPMENT
Segmented body; poisonous fangs; sensitive antennae

WEAKNESS
Dries up without humidity

FACT
Centipede poison paralyzes prey so that it becomes numb to sensory information.

AUTOMATIC INJECTION
Pinchers inject pressure-released poison into anything caught in centipedes' clutches.

DARK SCOPE
Centipedes' antennae sense vibrations and enable them to locate their prey in pitch darkness.

ELEVATOR EYES
Poison frogs blink by lowering their bulging eyes into their sockets. The pressure also helps them swallow.

WARNING SIGN
Vivid coloring lets predators know these frogs are poisonous—stay away!

SUPERPOWER
Toxic touch

EQUIPMENT
Long fingers; jumping legs; bright warning coloration

WEAKNESS
Thin skin that dehydrates quickly

FACT
Poison frog fathers pee on egg nests to keep their babies moist until they hatch.

SNACK TIME
Mother frogs feed unfertilized eggs to their tadpoles, laying the eggs in the tadpoles' pools for easy access.

SLIME SHIELD
Frogs' slime layer helps them absorb water from the air and protects them from water loss.

GEOGRAPHY
Nicaragua, Panama, Costa Rica

HABITAT
Hops around in forest-floor leaf litter, on trees, and in bromeliads

COLORFUL CHEMIST

Small poison frogs (also called poison-arrow frogs) hunt in broad daylight, fearlessly flashing their bright colors before would-be predators. Why so bold? These tiny amphibians produce one of the world's deadliest poisons. Any snake foolish enough to try to eat a poison frog will spit it out, then writhe or fall into a coma (sometimes for hours) before recovering from a single tiny taste.

ALLY

BROMELIADS
Rainforest bromeliads have cup-shaped leaves that hold water. They provide protected pools for developing tadpoles.

STRAWBERRY POISON FROG
Dendrobates pumilio

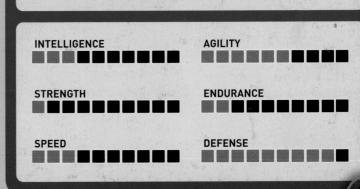

LENGTH: **1 INCH (2.5 CM)**   WEIGHT: **0.02 OUNCES (0.5 G)**

LIFE OR DEATH

FOOD POISONING
To gather ingredients for the deadly mix they wear on their skin, poison frogs eat poisonous beetles, mites, and ants. Once ingested, frogs chemically change these poisons, making them deadlier.

INTELLIGENCE	AGILITY
STRENGTH	ENDURANCE
SPEED	DEFENSE

SWARMING SCISSORS

Red-bellied piranhas have such fearsome reputations as people-eaters that locals wrap their legs with cloth for protection before walking in piranha-infested pools. Though these omnivores have been known to scavenge sizable dead or dying mammals, piranhas only attack large healthy prey when food is scarce. They gather in schools of ten to 100—more for protection than attack.

GEOGRAPHY
Rivers of the Guianas; Amazon and Paraná-Paraguay river basins

HABITAT
Swarms in ponds, flooded forests, and creeks

RED-BELLIED PIRANHA
Pygocentrus nattereri

LENGTH: **5 INCHES (13 CM)**   WEIGHT: **2.5 POUNDS (1 KG)**

INTELLIGENCE
■■■■■■■■■■■■

AGILITY
■■■■■■■■■■■■

STRENGTH
■■■■■■■■■■

ENDURANCE
■■■■■■■■■■

SPEED
■■■■■■■■■

EVASION
■■■■■■■■■■

ENEMIES

BOTOS
Amazon river dolphins are adept at navigating flooded forests and shrinking pools, where piranha schools are often trapped.

CAIMANS
These many-toothed alligators have tough skin and no fear of sharp piranha teeth. They readily seek out piranha snacks.

IN ACTION

FEEDING FRENZY
Red-bellied piranha schools are the industrial-strength vacuums of rainforest rivers. They suck up other fish, leaves, fruit, seeds, insects, and dead animals.

BUILT-IN AMP

Piranhas create sound by contracting muscles next to their air bladders. The bladders amplify noise, making it easier for other fish to hear.

SUPERPOWER
Group attack and defense

EQUIPMENT
Flat body; sharp interlocking teeth; sonic muscles

WEAKNESS
Inflexible eyes (piranhas are nearsighted)

FACT
Smaller piranhas attack more aggressively than larger ones.

SHEAR GENIUS

Razor-sharp teeth cut out bits of meat like scissors. Piranhas stay sharp by growing replacement teeth every four months.

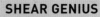

SIXTH SENSE

Muscles along a piranha's sides sense vibrations from changing currents and other fish.

PERFECT FIT

Cusps on each tooth fit together when the jaws are closed. They keep food from floating away.

SPEEDY BYPASS

Since blood is already liquid, it can be digested quickly, providing vampire bats with almost instant energy.

HEAT DETECTION

Heat-seeking noses help bats on the hunt by sensing blood vessels near the surface of prey's skin.

SUPERPOWERS

Superleaping ability; chemically enhanced saliva

EQUIPMENT

Heat-sensitive nose; grooved, lapping tongue

WEAKNESS

Will die within three days without food

FACT

To avoid becoming too heavy to fly after large meals, bats often urinate while eating.

SIPHON SUCTION

Bats don't suck blood—they lap it up. Two grooves on their tongues help keep the blood flowing into their mouths.

GYMNASTIC ACTION

Strong upper bodies let bats leap, cartwheel, or jerk sideways to avoid being squashed by large prey.

GEOGRAPHY

Mexico through the western coast of South America

HABITAT

Hangs out in caves, tree hollows, and abandoned buildings

BLOOD WRAITH

The stuff of legend, tiny vampire bats are versatile, fierce, and opportunistic. They are the only animals able to leap vertically into flight, and they're one of three bat species that eat blood exclusively. Feared for spreading rabies, yet valued for chemicals in their saliva, vampire bats have earned their creepy reputation by stealthily lapping the blood of their prey.

TOOL TIME

DSPA

Bat saliva contains draculin, which keeps blood from clotting. Doctors use DSPA derived from bat saliva to prevent brain clots.

PREY

COWS

Like some humans, vampire bats prefer their beef rare. They sneak up on cows at night and drain fresh blood while the cows sleep.

CHICKENS

After painlessly slicing a chicken's foot, a bat will feed on the trickle of blood. Repeat visits can weaken and kill the bird.

RODENTS

Before humans introduced cows into rainforest areas, bats got the majority of their mammal blood from rodents.

COMMON VAMPIRE BAT
Desmodus rotunda

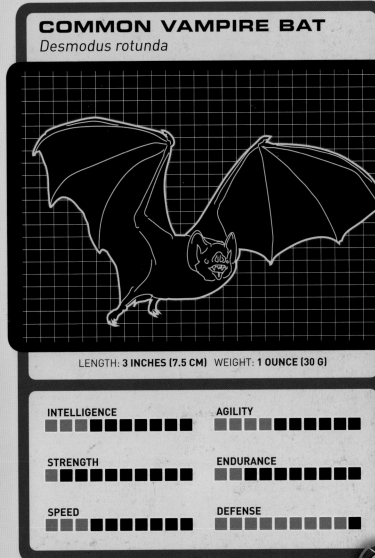

LENGTH: **3 INCHES (7.5 CM)**   WEIGHT: **1 OUNCE (30 G)**

INTELLIGENCE

AGILITY

STRENGTH

ENDURANCE

SPEED

DEFENSE

DRESSED TO KILL

Tigers' size and bright, distinctive markings give an obvious warning to anything prowling nearby—steer clear! These hungry hunters are the largest cats in the world and will not hesitate to attack, whether in defense of their territory or for food. In one year a single tiger may eat 50 to 60 large animals—that's 4 tons (3.5 tonnes) of meat!

GEOGRAPHY
India, China, Russia, Southeast Asia, Indonesia

HABITAT
Stalks through tropical and dry forests, grasslands, and mangroves

TIGER
Panthera tigris

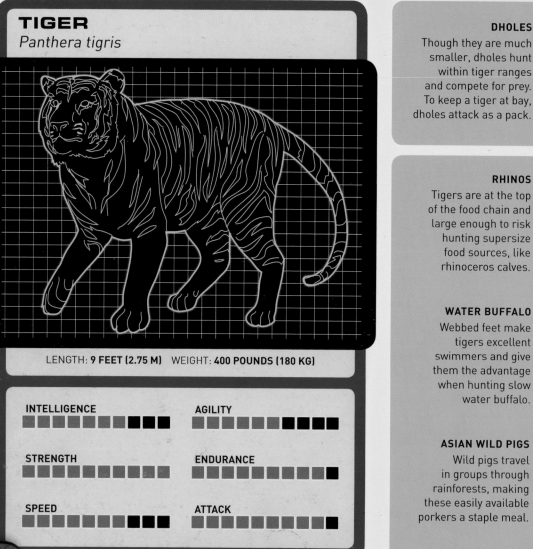

LENGTH: **9 FEET (2.75 M)**   WEIGHT: **400 POUNDS (180 KG)**

INTELLIGENCE
■■■■■■■□□□

AGILITY
■■■■■□□□□□

STRENGTH
■■■■■■■■■■

ENDURANCE
■■■■■■■■■□

SPEED
■■■■■■□□□

ATTACK
■■■■■■■■■□

ENEMY

DHOLES
Though they are much smaller, dholes hunt within tiger ranges and compete for prey. To keep a tiger at bay, dholes attack as a pack.

PREY

RHINOS
Tigers are at the top of the food chain and large enough to risk hunting supersize food sources, like rhinoceros calves.

WATER BUFFALO
Webbed feet make tigers excellent swimmers and give them the advantage when hunting slow water buffalo.

ASIAN WILD PIGS
Wild pigs travel in groups through rainforests, making these easily available porkers a staple meal.

ULTRASOUND
Large, swiveling ears hear sounds five to ten times higher in pitch than humans can hear.

DEADLY DAGGERS
Tigers' canines can grow up to 3 inches (7.5 cm) long and have gaps in the back that allow them to sink deeper into flesh.

QUANTUM LEAP
Strong hind legs can propel a tiger through the air 26 feet (8 m) in a single pounce.

SUPERPOWER
Peerless patience (tigers can stalk prey for more than an hour)

EQUIPMENT
Sharp claws; long canine teeth; webbed paws; sensitive ears

WEAKNESS
Slow over long distances

FACT
Tigers can swim fully submerged to attack prey from underneath.

SURE FOOTING
Long hairs along tigers' ankles sense surroundings and help them place their feet silently, without looking.

HIDE AND SEEK

The jungles of the rainforest house innumerable hungry mouths—all of them on the verge of eating or being eaten. In this wild free-for-all, species with strategies for remaining undetected have the best chance of surviving until their next meal. Camouflage (looking like the natural surroundings) and mimicry (resembling a more dangerous animal or a part of another animal) are effective survival strategies.

EVIL TWIN

Imitation is the highest form of flattery—and a clever strategy for survival, too. Mimicking the traits of a more dangerous animal keeps many less harmful critters from being eaten. For example, nonpoisonous sanguine mimic frogs (bottom) closely resemble the toxic Ecuadorian poison frog (top).

HEADS OR TAILS

Many moth- and butterfly-wing patterns use mimicry to confuse both predators and prey. Often, these wing patterns look like teeth or giant eyes. The Goliath moth is the largest moth in the world, and it appears to have a big bird beak on each of its wings to keep it safe.

FLASH OF BRILLIANCE

Fooling the eye isn't just about blending in—another effective form of camouflage is all about dazzling. Bright, bold coloration protects flocks of lorikeets by confusing would-be predators and making it difficult for them to single out a single victim.

BARKING UP THE WRONG TREE

Asia's Omei tree frog is not only colored like tree bark, it also has bumpy skin that resembles the bark's rough texture.

SPIDER SENSE
The many hairs along these spiders' legs and bodies detect the movement of other creatures.

POP TOP
Spiders molt as they grow. After opening a hole in their exoskeleton, they crawl out from inside their old shell.

SUPERPOWERS
Large size; pouncing attack

EQUIPMENT
Eight strong legs; irritating hairs; poison-filled fangs

WEAKNESS
Bad eyesight (can only see a short distance in front of it)

FACT
Tarantulas can slowly regrow missing legs.

HOLLOW BLADES
Red venom-filled fangs poison that digests spi before it's eaten.

HAIR SPRAY
When provoked, these spiders fling stinging hairs that irritate their pursuers' eyes and skin.

GEOGRAPHY
Eastern Brazil

HABITAT
Creeps over rainforest floors

PINK MONSTER

Brazilian salmon pinks get their name from the rosy-tipped hairs that cover their bodies. One of the largest spiders in the world, these tarantulas fearlessly roam the forest floor looking for prey and aggressively attack anything they perceive as a threat. If they happen upon a nest, these bird eaters will gladly dine on the chicks of ground-dwelling birds.

PREY

FROGS
Brazilian salmon pinks don't eat birds often. They more commonly make meals of frogs, snakes, and insects.

ENEMY

STUNNING STINGERS
Brazilian salmon pinks are defenseless against small spider wasps. After paralyzing the spider with a sting, a wasp lays its eggs inside the spider's body. Once hatched, wasp larvae eat their way out.

BRAZILIAN SALMON PINK
Lasiodora parahybana

LEG SPAN: **10 INCHES (25 CM)**

INTELLIGENCE

AGILITY

STRENGTH

ENDURANCE

SPEED

ATTACK

BREATH TAKER

Green anacondas are the world's largest and most aquatic constrictors. With reported lengths of 38 feet (11.5 m) and top weights of 550 pounds (250 kg), it's no surprise that this snake's giant size has terrified many—so much so that its Tamil name translates to "elephant killer." Although these snakes don't kill elephants, they do swallow whole prey as long as 6 feet (2 m). That's bigger than the average adult man.

GREEN ANACONDA
Eunectes murinus

LENGTH: **20 FEET (6 M)**   WEIGHT: **330 POUNDS (150 KG)**

INTELLIGENCE	AGILITY
STRENGTH	ENDURANCE
SPEED	ATTACK

PREY

MARSH DEER
The average green anaconda is 20 feet (6 m) long and has no problem swallowing marsh deer that measure 6 feet (2 m).

SHARP-SPINED CATFISH
Anacondas spend most of their time in the water, so it's no surprise that they like to eat large river animals such as sharp-spined catfish.

PECCARIES
Anacondas snare peccaries with a single bite. The snakes then wrap around their piglike prey, tightening their coils each time the peccaries exhale.

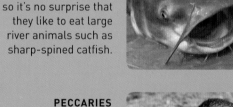

CAIMANS
In epic river battles that pit caimans' snapping jaws against anacondas' constricting coils, huge anacondas usually come out on top.

FLOTATION DEVICE
Naturally buoyant, anacondas swim the same way they move on land—by wriggling their long bodies.

STINK SHIELD
Anacondas produce an odor that prevents ticks and mites from feeding on them.

CONTACT LENS
Clear scales called brille cover anacondas' eyes to tightly seal out both air and water.

SNORKEL TUBE
Windpipes extend to the front of the mouth, allowing snakes to breathe while they swallow meals whole, which can take hours.

SUPERPOWERS
Supersize; supreme swimming

EQUIPMENT
Six rows of hooking teeth; elastic jaws; strong, squeezing coils

WEAKNESS
Overheats easily in the dry season

FACT
Anacondas "hear" by sensing vibrations around them with their jawbones.

SUPERPOWER
Daredevil leaps and glides

EQUIPMENT
Tiny claws; gliding membrane; long bushy tail

WEAKNESS
Cold intolerance (sugar gliders must hibernate on cold days)

FACT
Marsupial gliders carry young in pouches that protect their babies from the impact of landing.

STEERING RODS
Gliders steer like superheroes by dipping their arms to go left or right or even to make U-turns.

HAIR-RAISING
Each strand of fur helps increase lift, keeping the marsupial airborne longer.

STRAIGHT SHOOTER
Bushy glider tails work like rudders to create drag and keep flyers facing forward.

THUMBS-UP
Gliders' wing tips are connected to their thumbs. Pointing their thumbs up angles their skin flaps for smooth sailing.

GEOGRAPHY

New Guinea; northern and eastern Australia

HABITAT

Glides through rainforest midstories

HIGH FLYER

It takes a lot of time to climb up and down trees, especially if you live in the high-rise canopy of the rainforest. Sugar gliders cut down on their commute by simply vaulting from tree to tree. Special skin flaps beneath their arms extend like wings to increase hang time and keep these gliders airborne for as far as 135 feet (40 m) per flight.

PREY

PAPUAN WEEVILS

Sugar gliders live off sap and nectar but often add crunch to their diet by munching on insects such as Papuan weevils.

SUGAR GLIDER
Petaurus breviceps

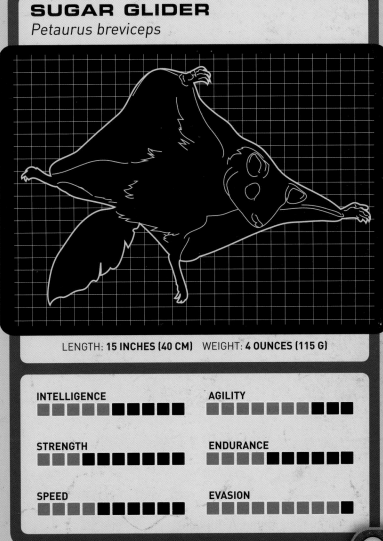

LENGTH: **15 INCHES (40 CM)**   WEIGHT: **4 OUNCES (115 G)**

TOOL TIME

WONDER WING

A sugar glider's patagium (the skin connected to the arm) extends to create a thin "wing" perfect for gliding. When not in use, the flap of skin folds up neatly so it doesn't get caught on branches.

INTELLIGENCE
■■■■■■□■■■

AGILITY
■■■■■■■■□□

STRENGTH
■■■■□■■■■■

ENDURANCE
■■■■■□■■■■

SPEED
■■■■■□■■■■

EVASION
■■■■■■■□□□

TALONS OF TERROR

The largest eagle in the world is no gentle giant. With talons up to 5 inches (13 cm) long, ankles thicker than a child's wrist, and a wingspan measuring up to 7 feet (2.25 m), this king of the sky can handily capture animals as large as it is. While holding its victim aloft, a harpy eagle will deliver a killing stab to the heart of its prey using specialized piercing talons.

GEOGRAPHY
Southeastern Mexico, across Amazon river basin, to southern Brazil

HABITAT
Swoops in tropical forest canopies and understories

HARPY EAGLE
Harpia harpyja

LENGTH: **3 FEET (1 M)** WEIGHT: **16 POUNDS (7.25 KG)**

INTELLIGENCE ■■■■■■■■■■

AGILITY ■■■■■■■■■■

STRENGTH ■■■■■■■■■■

ENDURANCE ■■■■■■■■■■

SPEED ■■■■■■■■■■

EVASION ■■■■■■■■■■

HOWLER MONKEYS
Investigations of debris beneath harpy eagles' nests have revealed howler monkey bones—evidence of many monkey meals.

PREY

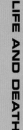

LIFE AND DEATH

AMBUSH HUNTERS
Harpy eagles prefer to sit perfectly still in trees until they spot their victims. Once they have sighted their prey, the eagles drop down and give chase through the trees, with claws extended.

FARSIGHTED

Harpy eagles can spot a small mouse from 660 feet (200 m) away.

PRECISION PIERCING

The death blow of a harpy eagle leaves a puncture wound in the victim's chest that measures only 0.5 inches (13 mm).

CRUSHER BLADES

Harpy eagles can exert enough pressure with their claws to smash bones and instantly kill prey.

SUPERPOWERS

Extreme vision; piercing talons

EQUIPMENT

Head crest; steering tail; massive claws

WEAKNESS

Fixed eyes (must move head to look in other directions)

FACT

Harpies reach gliding speeds of up to 50 miles (80 km) per hour.

REAR SPOILER

Short, broad tails increase maneuverability for weaving through dense treetops.

41

SUPERPOWERS
Flexibility; echolocation (using reflected sound waves to locate and identify objects)

EQUIPMENT
Long-toothed snout; large flippers and flukes; small eyes

WEAKNESS
Can only survive in freshwater

FACT
River dolphins are born gray and turn pink with age.

RUBBERNECKER
River dolphins' neck bones are connected by stretchy ligaments, allowing their heads to bend 90 degrees from side to side.

"HIGH SIX!"
River dolphins' wide flippers are modified hands. The boto is the only dolphin species with a sixth "finger" bone.

SAWTOOTH
Botos grasp and chew prey with inflexible jaws that contain up to 70 teeth.

HALF-TIME
One half of a river dolphin's brain can sleep while the other is awake.

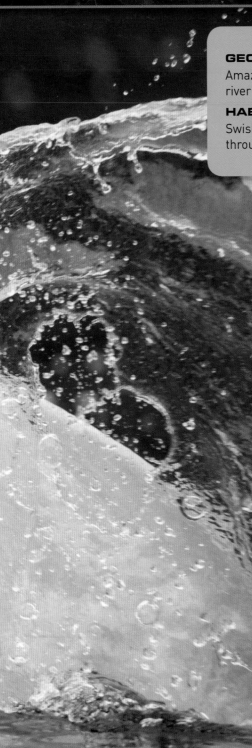

GEOGRAPHY
Amazonian and Orinoco river systems

HABITAT
Swishes along rivers and through flooded forests

RIVER ROVER

Pink-skinned botos, or Amazon river dolphins, won't win any beauty contests, but these creatures could capture top prizes for hunting. Botos comb open waters and flooded forests for fish, their lithe movements helping them catch prey. This flexibility also aids in defense: when evading capture, they turn and twist quickly and crazily, making them difficult to track.

ENEMY

HUMANS
Although they share space with hunters as fierce as anacondas and jaguars, botos are killed most often when snared in fishing nets.

PREY

PIRANHAS
Amazon river dolphins rule rainforest waters. They enjoy more than 50 species of fish, including dangerous and sharp-toothed piranhas.

TURTLES
Botos are adept at navigating flooded forest floors. They hunt turtles in areas other river animals can't reach.

CRABS
In murky waters, river dolphins locate hiding crabs by emitting sounds that bounce back and reveal crabs' locations.

BOTO
Inia geoffrensis

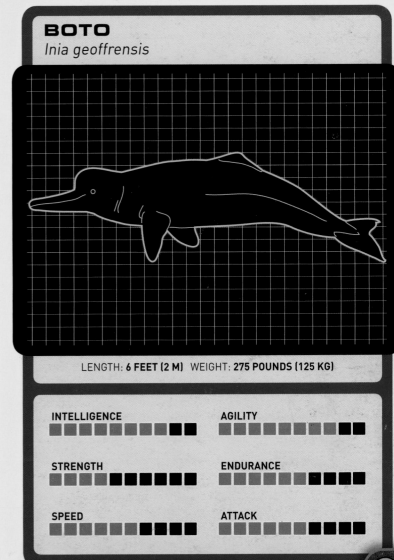

LENGTH: **6 FEET (2 M)**   WEIGHT: **275 POUNDS (125 KG)**

INTELLIGENCE	AGILITY
STRENGTH	ENDURANCE
SPEED	ATTACK

RAINFOREST CHALLENGE

From the storm-swept canopy, down the armored trunks of the midstory, to the disease-filled understory and flooded forest floor, a gauntlet of challenges awaits rainforest inhabitants at every level. In this extreme environment, staying alive takes special skills—and survival is not a game.

RAINFOREST LEVELS

EMERGENT LAYER

CANOPY

MIDSTORY

UNDERSTORY

FLOOR

STRANGLER FIGS

PITCHER PLANTS

LUNGFISH

TERRIFYING TREES

HIGH WATERS

Amazon waters reportedly flood as high as 40 feet (12 m) in the wet season and send animals into the trees. In the dry season, waters recede, stranding fish in isolated ponds. Lungfish breathe air and move from pool to shrinking pool to survive.

SHADOWLANDS

Most animals live in the canopy, where food and light are plentiful. As little as 1 percent of available sunlight filters through the canopy, midstory, and understory to the barren forest floor. Down in the dark, decomposers such as fungi, insects, and bacteria survive in the deep leaf layer.

Many hungry plant species have developed alternative energy plans and treacherous defenses. Strangler figs wrap around other trees and live off them like parasites. Pitcher plants trap and eat insects. Still other plants grow spikes and thorns to keep invaders at bay.

MUD HOLES

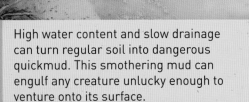

High water content and slow drainage can turn regular soil into dangerous quickmud. This smothering mud can engulf any creature unlucky enough to venture onto its surface.

BANYAN TREES

STORM WARNING

Tropical cyclones whip through Australasian rainforests. Violent storms can knock out up to one-third of a forest's trees. Banyan trees grow buttresses (reinforcing trunks) for stability. Even so, winds up to 125 miles (200 km) per hour wipe out bats, birds, and other canopy dwellers.

GERM FACTORY

Warm, humid rainforest temperatures create perfect breeding grounds for insects, bacteria, fungi, and other disease-causing organisms. Dark-colored animals, such as black leopards and jaguars, are more common in rainforests because the same trait that makes fur black may also provide better defenses against viruses.

BLACK JAGUARS

GLOSSARY

algae Plantlike organisms that grow in water or damp conditions. Green algae grows in the fur of sloths and provides camouflage.

ally An animal that helps another animal, usually to the mutual benefit of both.

Amazon The Amazon River, one of the world's largest rivers, is about 4,000 miles (6,437 km) long. It is located in northern South America and flows from the Peruvian Andes to the Atlantic Ocean in northern Brazil. The Amazon basin is the area of South America drained by the Amazon River. It stretches from northern Brazil into Venezuela, Colombia, Ecuador, Peru, and Bolivia and is home to the largest rainforest in the world.

amphibian An animal that is able to live both on land and in water.

antenna One of a pair of slender, movable, and segmented sensory organs on the head of an arthropod. Arthropods, such as insects or crabs, use their antennae to sense movement, temperature, smells, or even tastes.

aquatic Growing or living in freshwater or saltwater. Aquatic animals live in water for most or all of their lives.

biodiversity The variety of living organisms in an environment, as indicated by numbers of different species of plants and animals. Rainforests are the most biologically diverse environments in the world.

bromeliad One of a family of flowering plants that is able to store water in cups formed by tightly overlapping leaf bases. Pools of water that form in bromeliads make ideal nursery ponds for developing tadpoles.

buoyant Capable of floating easily in water.

camouflage A physical characteristic that helps an animal blend into its environment to hide from predators.

canine teeth The two pairs of pointed teeth on the top and bottom of the mouth. Most meat eaters have long, sharp canines that help them tear flesh.

canopy The primary layer of the rainforest made up of the crowns of trees. Leaves and branches intersect to catch most of the sunlight and form a roof over the layers below. The canopy is home to many animals, including monkeys, snakes, birds, and frogs.

counterbalance A weight that balances another. A basilisk lizard's tail balances the weight of its body so that the lizard doesn't tip over when running.

deciduous Trees and shrubs that lose their leaves seasonally. Deciduous forests are made up of plants that shed their leaves and become dormant during cold seasons. Most rainforests are not considered deciduous. They feature broad-leaved trees that grow continuously.

draculin A substance found in vampire bat saliva that prevents blood from clotting. Draculin is stronger than any other known blood thinner. Its derivative, DSPA, is in medications prescribed for both heart attack and stroke patients.

drag In physics, something that slows down motion. Drag can be produced by moving against air or water. Sugar gliders are slowed down by drag when jumping through the air from tree to tree.

echolocation A process for navigating or sensing the location of objects (such as prey) by reflecting sound waves. Dolphins emit clicking sounds that bounce off solid forms and echo back. Using this process, dolphins can identify the location, size, and shape of unseen objects. Echolocation is important to many marine animals because it allows them to hunt and navigate in dark or murky waters.

emergent layer The topmost layer of the rainforest made up of widely spaced trees that extend above the canopy.

enemy An animal that is harmful or has a negative relationship with another animal.

fang One of a pair of long, sharp teeth used by animals to grasp, seize, or tear. Many snakes have fangs that are hollow and poison filled.

fluke The back "fin" of a dolphin or whale tail. Flukes move up and down to propel through water and also act as rudders, or stabilizers.

forest floor The bottommost layer of the rainforest. It receives very little sunlight and contains plants adapted to low light as well as decaying plant and animal matter. It is home to many insects, reptiles, and a few mammals that do not dwell in trees.

Guianas A region of South America including Suriname, Guyana, and French Guiana.

habitat The environment where an animal is best suited to live in the wild.

hibernate To spend the winter in a sleeping or resting state. Hibernating animals conserve energy by lowering respiratory, metabolic, and heart rates, as well as their temperature.

infrared Light or energy waves situated beyond the spectrum visible to humans on the red end. Infrared waves are often experienced as heat. Emerald green boas have sensory organs near their mouths that detect the heat waves and help them locate predators or prey.

ligament A tough band of flexible tissue that connects bones or holds organs in place.

mangrove An area of dense trees or shrubs that grow in salty marshes or shallow saltwater, such as flooded rainforests.

marsupial An order of mammals, including opossums, wombats, and kangaroos, that have pouches to carry their young. Sugar gliders have pouches that carry their young and protect them from impact when they land.

metabolism The process in living organisms whereby energy is built up and stored or food is broken down and transformed into the energy that the organism needs to move, eat, and otherwise function.

midstory The middle layer of the rainforest between the canopy and the understory. The midstory consists of midsize trees and shrubs. It is not as sunny as the canopy.

molting The periodic shedding of a creature's outer layer. The cast-off shell or skin is replaced by new growth. Spiders such as the Brazilian salmon pink bird eater molt many times throughout their lives.

omnivore An animal that eats both plant and animal food sources.

Orinoco The Orinoco River is one of the largest rivers in South America. It flows through most of Venezuela, part of Colombia, a small portion of the Guianas, and then empties into the Atlantic Ocean. The Orinoco basin extends from the Andes mountain range to the edge of the Guianas.

Paraná-Paraguay The second-largest river system in South America, the Paraná-Paraguay flows through Argentina, Paraguay, and Brazil.

patagium The fold of skin, or membrane, extending from the body and connecting the front and back limbs of bats and gliding mammals such as sugar gliders.

predator An animal that hunts other animals for the food it needs to survive.

prehensile A physical trait that is adapted for holding or grasping. For instance, animals like tamanduas and snakes have tails they wrap around branches to hold themselves in place.

prey Animals that are hunted and eaten by other animals.

rainforest A region with dense tree coverage that receives over 8 feet (2.5 m) of rain a year. Home to more than half of the animal species living on Earth, rainforests once covered 14 percent of the world's surface but now cover 6 percent.

savanna A region with tropical or subtropical weather, wide grasslands, and scattered trees.

scrubland An area characterized by the presence of shrubs, grasses, and herbs.

shoal A school or group of fish. Piranhas cluster in shoals of ten to one hundred fish.

siphon A tube that draws liquid.

sonic Anything that relates to, produces, or uses sound waves. Lines of muscle on the sides of piranhas pick up sonic vibrations, allowing them to "hear" approaching fish.

subtropical The geographical regions bordering the tropical zone between twenty and 40 degrees in both latitudes. Subtropical regions have warm winters and hot summers.

termite A soft-bodied insect that lives in colonies and feeds on wood. Termites eat mostly dead wood in rainforests.

territory An area that is occupied and defended by an animal or group of animals. Jaguar males do not like to share territory with other males but will share with females.

tropical The geographical region between the two parallel latitudes that lie 23.5 degrees north and south of the equator. Tropical rainforests are found near the equator in Asia, Australia, Africa, South America, Central America, Mexico, and on the Pacific Islands. Average temperatures in the tropical rainforest are higher than 76°F (26°C) most of the year.

understory The layer of the rainforest between the midstory and the forest floor. The understory is characterized by shorter trees such as palms and young saplings. Birds and reptiles live at this level along with predators such as constrictors and jaguars.

venom A poisonous substance produced by snakes, spiders, and other insects that can be injected by biting or stinging into the tissue of prey to paralyze or kill.

CREDITS

All illustrations by **Liberum Donum** (Juan Calle, Santiago Calle, Andres Penagos).

All images courtesy of **Shutterstock** unless noted below.
Age Fotostock: 22 bottom
Alamy: 10 main; 23 main; 45 far bottom right
Corbis: 31 main
Getty: front cover; 20 main
iStock: 27 main; 34 main; 44 far top right; 45 far top left; 45 (unfolded) far left and far right
Minden Pictures: 24 main (Thomas Marent); 38 main (Scott Linstead); 40 bottom (Pete Oxford); 41 main (Tui De Roy); 42 main (Kevin Schafer)
National Geographic Image Collection: 14 main (Roy Toft); 37 main (Claus Meyer)
Photolibrary: 9 main (Joe McDonald)
Science Photo Library: 18 bottom (Stan Wayman/ Photo Researchers, Inc.)

ACKNOWLEDGMENTS

Special thanks to Jacqueline Aaron, Karen Clarke, Bret Hansen, Sheila Masson, Susan McCombs, and Marisa Solís.